T0303819

CHISWICK
IN
50
BUILDINGS

LUCY McMURDO

AMBERLEY

In memory of my early childhood

First published 2021

Amberley Publishing, The Hill, Stroud
Gloucestershire GL5 4EP

www.amberley-books.com

British Library Cataloguing in Publication Data.
A catalogue record for this book is available from the British Library.

ISBN 978 1 4456 9960 8 (print)
ISBN 978 1 4456 9961 5 (ebook)

Typesetting by Aura Technology and Software Services, India.
Printed in Great Britain.

Contents

Map   4

Key   5

Introduction   7

The 50 Buildings   10

About the Author   95

Acknowledgements   96

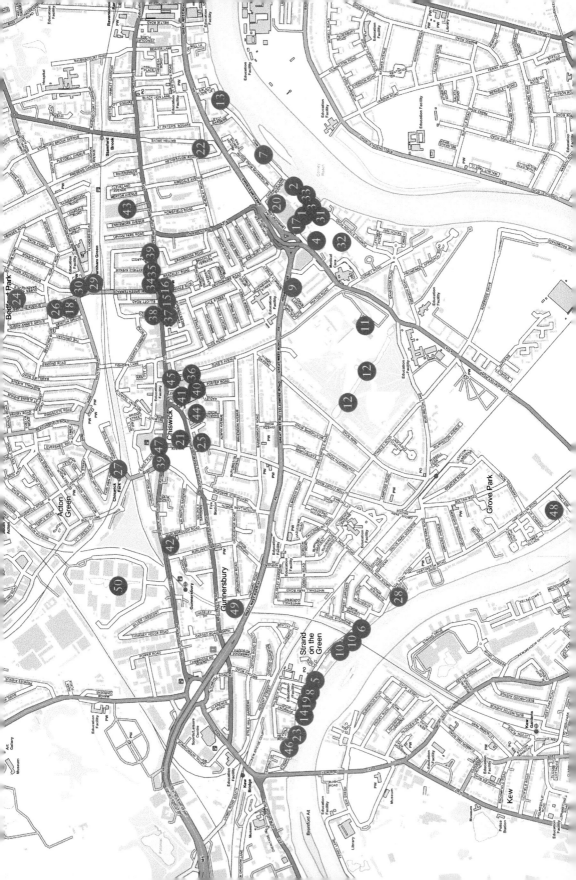

Key

1. Old Burlington, Nos 1–2 Church Street
2. Bedford and Eynham Houses, Chiswick Mall
3. Church Street: The Old Vicarage, Lamb Cottage and Wistaria House
4. Chiswick Square and the George & Devonshire Pub, Burlington Lane
5. Ship House and Dutch House, Nos 56 and 60 Strand on the Green
6. Hopkin Morris Cottages, Strand on the Green
7. Walpole House, Chiswick Mall
8. Zoffany House, No. 65 Strand on the Green
9. Hogarth House, Hogarth Lane
10. Riverside Pubs: The City Barge and Bulls Head, Strand on the Green
11. Chiswick House, Burlington Lane
12. Chiswick House Gardens and Grounds
13. Hammersmith Terrace
14. Riverside Buildings, Strand on the Green
15. George IV Public House, No. 185 Chiswick High Road
16. Foster Books, No. 183 Chiswick High Road
17. The Lamb Brewery, off Church Street
18. Bedford House, The Avenue, Bedford Park
19. Zachary House, No. 70 Strand on the Green
20. Fuller's Griffin Brewery, Great West Road, Chiswick Lane; Mawson Arms and the Fox & Hounds, Mawson Lane
21. Christ Church, Turnham Green
22. British Grove Studios, No. 20 British Grove
23. The Steam Packet Public House, No. 85 Strand on the Green
24. Bedford Park and No. 3 Blenheim Road
25. Former Chiswick Town Hall, Heathfield Terrace
26. London Buddhist Vihara – former Bedford Park Club – The Avenue, Bedford Park
27. Chiswick Park Station, Bollo Lane and Acton Lane
28. Nos 68–74 Grove Park Road
29. Tabard Inn and Chiswick Playhouse, Bath Road
30. St Michael and All Angels Church, Bath Road
31. St Nicholas Church, Church Street
32. St Nicholas Churchyard and Burial Ground
33. Said House, Chiswick Mall
34. High Road House, Nos 162–170 Chiswick High Road
35. The Old Cinema, No. 160 Chiswick High Road
36. Chiswick Public Library, No. 1 Duke's Avenue
37. The Fire Station, No. 197 Chiswick High Road
38. The Crown Public House, No. 210 Chiswick High Road

39. Ancient Inns, Chiswick High Road
40. Sanderson's and Barley Mow Passage
41. The Voysey Building, Barley Mow Passage
42. Harold Pinter's Home, No. 373 Chiswick High Road
43. Former Tram Depot and Power House, Nos 70–72 Chiswick High Road
44. Former Army and Navy Furniture Depository, Heathfield Terrace
45. Our Lady of Grace and St Edward, No. 247 Chiswick High Road
46. Former Pier House Laundry, Nos 86–94 Strand on the Green
47. Chiswick Empire, Nos 414–424 Chiswick High Road
48. Chiswick Quay
49. The Cathedral of the Nativity of the Most Holy Mother of God and the Royal Martyrs, No. 57 Harvard Road
50. Chiswick Park, No. 566 Chiswick High Road

Introduction

Chiswick's reputation as one of London's most popular villages is hardly surprising considering its splendid riverside location and easy access into town. For more than 2,000 years it has lain on the main route west from London and has always been an extremely busy thoroughfare lined with inns and taverns. This remains a feature of the district today and no one could possibly go hungry along Chiswick High Road, which has an extensive array of pubs, cafés, restaurants and bars. Chiswick is renowned for its green, leafy rural ambiance, although it is a thriving commercial centre too. In the nineteenth century it was an area of market gardens and home to the Horticultural Society of London, but with the march of industrialisation came enormous population growth, and former rural land was sold for housing development. The coming of the railway in the 1840s transformed Chiswick's villages – Turnham Green, Old Chiswick, Strand on the Green and Little Sutton – into a London suburb, giving residents the opportunity to work locally or commute to central London.

Throughout its history Chiswick has been attractive to Londoners, artists, aristocrats and the affluent as somewhere to buy a second home, often alongside the river. In 1749 Hogarth purchased his 'little box in the country' that could be easily accessed by water and road and where he could enjoy the clean, sweet local air. Chiswick's charms have remained largely unchanged, so it is no wonder that so many creative personalities, professionals and even royalty (Edward VII before he was crowned king) have settled in the village at one time or another. It is impossible to list them all here, but readers will come across a selection of their stories within the book.

Perhaps Chiswick's most celebrated resident is the 3rd Earl of Burlington, who in the 1720s built the Palladian-style Chiswick House, assisted by his protégé William Kent. The house is undoubtedly one of Chiswick's greatest treasures not only for its architecture and sumptuous interiors but also for its stunning grounds full of statuary, ornamental buildings, Grade I listed conservatory and water features, and is considered to be the birthplace of the English landscape movement. The estate hosts many events during the year including Lightopia, a winter light trail, and the highly acclaimed annual Camellia Show. Its café won the 2011 RIBA London Building of the Year Award and lies to the east of the main house in an area once home to stables.

From the early eighteenth century Chiswick became closely associated with the brewing industry and home to the Lamb and Griffin breweries.

The Lamb closed down in 1920 but the Griffin Brewery, originally owned by Fuller, Smith & Turner, still operates on its original site. It is now owned by Japanese brewers Asahi, who continue to brew Fullers beers and run regular tours of the brewery where visitors learn about the brewing process and sample some of the company's internationally renowned beers.

During the nineteenth century Chiswick underwent much change. New industries were established such as Sanderson's, the wallpaper manufacturer, a plethora of laundries sprung up throughout the district catering for Chiswick's ever-increasing population as well as London's grand houses and hotels, and Thornycroft & Co. set up its successful ship and torpedo building business at Chiswick Wharf. As industrialisation took its hold, Chiswick's long-established fishing industry and riverside trades went into decline and had all but disappeared by the early 1900s.

The year 1875 saw work commence on Britain's first garden suburb: Bedford Park. Located in Chiswick's northern corner, it covered what had once been market gardens and orchards and was developed by Jonathan Carr, a follower of the Arts and Craft movement. He engaged a succession of architects (including R. Norman Shaw) to design the estate's housing, church, communal buildings and to layout the infrastructure. It was the vision of these men that created the beautiful tree-lined avenues and Bedford Park's very handsome housing, mainly in the Queen Anne Revival style. During the twentieth century when the suburb was under threat of unwanted development the poet laureate Sir John Betjeman carried out a successful campaign to save the suburb and this led to Bedford Park's designation as a conservation area. Further protection of the suburb was established in 1970 when many of the houses were awarded listed status. Bedford Park today is a thriving neighbourhood and is the venue for several festivals throughout the year including the celebrated Chiswick Book Festival that takes place in September.

Chiswick has always been a hub for culture and many of its buildings have been and are still used regularly for concerts, lectures, ballet, yoga and pilates classes. In the early twentieth century the High Road was alive with cinema and music hall entertainment and even had its own theatre, the Empire, famous throughout London for its popular artistes such as Laurel and Hardy and for its drama and variety acts. Nowadays there is just one theatre: the Chiswick Playhouse, located above the Tabard Inn. It is a small and intimate space loved by many for its exciting programme of contemporary and experimental productions.

The construction in the mid-twentieth century of the major A4 route sliced Chiswick into two distinct areas: the older riverside villages in the south around Chiswick Mall and Strand on the Green, and Chiswick High Road and Turnham Green in the north. Most of the area's earliest buildings are clustered around Church Street in Old Chiswick, while much of the newer Victorian housing stock is found on and around Chiswick High Road. It is fortunate that in recent years many parts of Chiswick have been designated conservation areas as this had prevented unsightly developments from going ahead. More importantly it has ensured that Chiswick's unique features and picturesque settings, such as those beside the river, remain unspoilt. The Thames continues to be a major attraction of the area and thousands line its banks each spring to watch the Oxford and Cambridge Boat Race that finishes its course at Chiswick Bridge.

I have really enjoyed the past few months exploring Chiswick, learning about its past and meeting its residents. It has a wonderful village ambiance, magnificent architecture (some of it dating to the fifteenth century), a flourishing shopping centre and historic riverside pubs. There is certainly something here for all to enjoy either as resident or visitor, guaranteeing Chiswick's continuing appeal as one of the capital's most fashionable destinations.

How to Use This Book

In accordance with the *50 Buildings* series, the buildings appear in chronological order according to the time of their original construction.

Please note that the map identifies each building by a number that corresponds to the numbers used in the text.

The 50 Buildings

1. Old Burlington, Nos 1–2 Church Street

It is fitting that the first building of this book, Old Burlington, is found in one of Chiswick's most ancient settlements situated right beside the River Thames. The area's earliest community, dependent upon fishing, had grown up alongside the riverbank and later, its residents were involved in a range of industries including boatbuilding, brewing and basketmaking. In time, dwellings spread from Chiswick Mall and Chiswick Wharf into Church Street, which became Old Chiswick's main high street. Filled with village shops, a couple of pubs and a range of cottages and houses, Church Street extended northwards to Burlington Lane where it joined the original Roman road going west from London.

Old Burlington is easy to spot: a pretty black and white half-timbered building with a projecting upper storey, typical of the Tudor and Elizabethan age.

Old Burlington. (© A. McMurdo)

Old Burlington.
(© A. McMurdo)

It is thought to be the oldest building in Chiswick, dating back to around the fifteenth or sixteenth centuries (an Elizabethan sixpence was discovered under the floorboards), and is said to have its own resident ghost, Percy, identified by his wide-brimmed hat. Undoubtedly, it has a long and interesting history.

Old Burlington was initially constructed as one building and for around 400 years functioned as a public house, one of several in Old Chiswick. By 1732 it was known as the Burlington Arms, taking its name from the Earl of Burlington, who owned nearby Chiswick House (q.v). If you were to peek inside this period house, you would marvel at its beautiful wood panelling and exposed oak beams along with its pretty walled courtyard garden and large double cellar. Today, located within the local conservation area and designated as an English Heritage listed property, Old Burlington is well protected, and no alterations can be made to the building without first obtaining listed building consent.

During the nineteenth century Old Burlington was occupied not only by the publican and his wife but also a carpenter, boatbuilder and fisherman. As the area became more industrialised and the riverside trades diminished these lodgers were replaced by a general servant, in keeping with the late Victorian age.

Station: Turnham Green

2. Bedford and Eynham Houses, Chiswick Mall

Chiswick Mall where Bedford House is located is certainly one of the village's most scenic parts. The site where Bedford House now stands was once a domestic brewhouse and in the eighteenth century brewer Thomas Mawson established his Griffin Brewery around it, which is still a key landmark of the area.

The first Bedford House was built in the seventeenth century by Edward Russell, the second son of the 4th Earl of Bedford, the head of one of England's most powerful families. In fact, the Russells have always been prominent, famous for their role in politics and in the navy. The Bedford Estates continue as a major central London landowner in Bloomsbury, and the family's country estate, Woburn Abbey in Bedfordshire, attracts thousands of visitors each year.

When Russell died in 1665 his house was sold to pay off debts and was then rebuilt in the early 1700s as one large dwelling and named Bedford House in his memory. The new luxurious building was handsome and constructed of brown brick in the Jacobean style. Over the years the house was altered on a number of occasions and at some point was divided into two separate dwellings – Bedford and Eynham Houses. If you stand on Chiswick Mall with your back to the River Thames you can see the former on the left and the latter on the right.

The houses share a central classical pediment and boast beautiful features such as a traceried fanlight, bow and dormer windows and attractive keystones. In the early nineteenth century John Sich, who founded the nearby Lamb Brewery, lived here with his family. Over the years, Bedford House was home to local historian Warwick Draper, a London Hospital physician, Sir Arthur Ellis, and in the mid-twentieth century to actors Michael Redgrave and Rachel Kempson and their young family. The children, Vanessa, Corin and Lynn, as well as several of their grandchildren, have continued in their parent's footsteps and remain celebrated actors today.

Designated a Grade II* listed building by English Heritage in 1951, Bedford House is an excellent example of early eighteenth-century architecture.

Stations: Turnham Green and Stamford Brook

Bedford House. (© A. McMurdo)

Eynham House. (© A. McMurdo)

3. Church Street: The Old Vicarage, Lamb Cottage and Wistaria House

The Old Vicarage is located at the junction of Chiswick Mall and Church Street right beside the River Thames. It is a striking house dating to the mid-1600s and like many within the vicinity has listed status. Right opposite St Nicholas Church (q.v.), it occupies a corner plot and is easily recognised because of its charming bow window facing the river. It was extended in the late nineteenth century when a Chapter House was built to house the vicar's large and growing family. However, the buildings were sold off and moved into private hands when a new vicarage was built in the 1970s.

Church Street itself is endowed with some delightful houses that date mainly from the seventeenth and eighteenth centuries and boast many interesting architectural features. Lamb Cottage, the former Lamb Tap public house beside Old Burlington, is noticeable for its weather-boarded façade, while Wistaria, as its name suggests, has walls covered by the climbing shrub. The hanging clusters of pale blue flowers on its frontage during the flowering season are a wonderful sight. It is no wonder that several members of the Sich family (who ran Old Chiswick's Lamb Brewery) chose to live in this charming street during the 1800s.

Station: Turnham Green

Left: The Old
Vicarage.
(© A. McMurdo)

Below: Lamb Cottage.
(© A. McMurdo)

Wistaria House. (© A. McMurdo)

4. Chiswick Square and the George & Devonshire Pub, Burlington Lane

Chiswick Square is a tiny enclave dominated by a very fine late seventeenth-century three-storey brown brick mansion: Boston House, flanked on either side by two houses of the period. The large forecourt in front of Boston House makes it an imposing setting, especially for a square of such small proportions. It is named after local resident Lord Boston (Earl of Grantham), who actually lived elsewhere in Chiswick. Legend claims that he murdered his adulterous wife, then buried her in the garden, leading to sightings of a seemingly terrified woman wandering in the grounds with her hands outstretched. Despite its apparent haunted status, the house later became a school for young ladies, and then a home for inebriated women. In the early 1900s it was taken over by a Roman Catholic sisterhood, the Sisters of Nazareth. Chiswick Products Ltd (CPL), famous for its Cherry Blossom Boot Polish, purchased the site in 1922. For the next fifty years Boston House was used as a social club for the company's female employees and the company installed a bowling green, sports pavilion and tennis courts in its grounds.

Above: Boston House. (© A. McMurdo)

Below: The George & Devonshire. (© A. McMurdo)

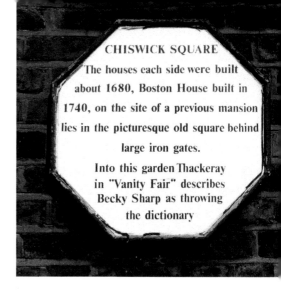

CHISWICK SQUARE
The houses each side were built about 1680, Boston House built in 1740, on the site of a previous mansion lies in the picturesque old square behind large iron gates.
Into this garden Thackeray in "Vanity Fair" describes Becky Sharp as throwing the dictionary

Chiswick Square plaque. (© A. McMurdo)

When CPL ultimately sold the premises the house underwent a complete refurbishment and was turned into private housing in the 1980s.

Sitting right beside Chiswick Square is the George & Devonshire public house, one of the earliest inns of the neighbourhood. 'The George', as it was originally known, was bought at the turn of the eighteenth century by Thomas Mawson, the brewer who founded Fuller, Smith & Turner. By the late 1700s productions of Shakespeare and other dramas were performed here by 'His Majesty's Servants' in what became known as the George Theatre. In the 1820s the pub changed its name to the George & Devonshire, alluding to the Duke of Devonshire, the owner of much of the surrounding land, at which point the duke's coat of arms was added to the pub sign.

Although not substantiated, local legend claims that during the eighteenth century contraband goods reached the George & Devonshire via a tunnel that stretched between the pub and the river.

Station: Turnham Green

5. Ship House and Dutch House, Nos 56 and 6c Strand on the Green

Strand on the Green is one of Chiswick's original villages and now designated a Conservation Area. Running alongside the River Thames, it is largely residential with little evidence of its former shops or industry. It is extremely picturesque with an assortment of tiny fishermen's cottages, terraced housing, public houses and charming Georgian houses.

Dating from the late eighteenth century Ship House was originally one of several public houses beside the riverbank. Attached to the much older Ship Cottage (1690), the pub was converted to a house in 1910. Typically, it attracted residents from the middle and professional classes and in the mid-twentieth century it became the home of the British psychiatrist, academic and Reith lecturer Professor George Carstairs. He was a good friend of the poet Dylan Thomas, who was known to have stayed in Ship Cottage from time to time.

Above left: Ship House. (© A. McMurdo)

Above right: Dutch House. (© A. McMurdo)

Just a little to the west one reaches a group of cottages attached to a house that stands out on account of its pretty shutters and gabled roof. Known as the Dutch House, between 1959 and 1964 this was the home of the film director John Guillermin, famous for films such as *King Kong Lives* (1986), and *The Towering Inferno* (1974).

Stations: Kew Bridge, Chiswick and Gunnersbury

6. Hopkin Morris Cottages, Strand on the Green

It is difficult to imagine today how Strand on the Green would have looked in times gone by, but we know that in its heyday the riverbank, reflecting employment in the area, was filled with boatbuilders' sheds, laundries, maltings and public houses, as well as residential accommodation. It was a busy waterfront with flights of steps up to the riverside roadway for visitors. The river path separated the Strand from its buildings and a number of tiny alleyways ran between the buildings and the road behind.

The charming Hopkin Morris Homes of Rest were erected at No. 84 Strand on the Green as homes for the poor in the seventeenth century. They were originally a thatched terrace of six one-room dwellings facing on to a small alley, Grove Row, that linked the riverside and Thames Road behind. In the 1720s, funded by public subscription, they were completely rebuilt as a modest one-storey brick range, but 200 years later the buildings were showing their age and in need of repair. Funding for their renovation was donated by the estate of Chiswick councillor and philanthropist B. Hopkin Morris, and at this time the

Hopkin Morris Cottages. (© A. McMurdo)

homes were extended and refurbished. They were ultimately renamed the Hopkin Morris Homes of Rest and the previous six units were transformed into three two-roomed houses, each with its own attractive front garden.

Since medieval times almshouses have been features of many UK towns and cities and were provided as homes for the elderly poor before the state pension was introduced in the early twentieth century. Up until the early sixteenth century they were administered by religious orders but following the Dissolution of the Monasteries in the 1530s many of the buildings were sold off to private landowners or simply fell into neglect. Fortunately, the City livery companies and craft guilds recognised the need to supply homes for the vulnerable, the poor and the elderly and stepped in to found 'hospitals' catering for their needs. Even today some of London's livery companies and guilds continue to manage almshouses, but the Hopkin Morris cottages have now passed into private hands.

Stations: Kew Bridge, Chiswick and Gunnersbury

7. Walpole House, Chiswick Mall

This imposing early eighteenth-century house sits on Chiswick Mall and has stunning views of the river. It is noted not only for its architectural features, dating to the sixteenth and seventeenth centuries, but also for its grand appearance,

Walpole House.
(© A. McMurdo)

Walpole House.
(© A. McMurdo)

and is one of only three buildings in Chiswick to have been assigned Grade 1 listed status by English Heritage.

Considering its position it is not surprising that Walpole House has been home to so many well-known residents. It owes its name to the Honourable Thomas Walpole MP (1727–1803), who was the nephew of England's first prime minister, Sir Robert Walpole, and lived here with his family in the late eighteenth century. Almost a century earlier it was home to one of Charles II's most beloved mistresses, Barbara Villiers (1640–1709), Lady Castelmaine, and latterly Duchess of Cleveland. During her life she had given birth to five illegitimate children of the king – three sons and two daughters. Her sons became dukes and the daughters married earls. Although during her lifetime she was considered a great beauty, when the duchess moved to Walpole House she was elderly and bloated from dropsy. She died shortly after, being buried in nearby St Nicholas Church (q.v.). In 1817 when Walpole House became an academy for young gentlemen, poet William Makepeace Thackeray studied here. It is said that he styled Miss Pinkerton's Seminary for Young Ladies on the academy when writing his famous book *Vanity Fair*. Towards the end of the century the house was purchased by John Thorneycroft, the local shipbuilder. During his tenure he built a workshop in the garden and it was here that his father's enormous sculpture of Boadicca in her chariot was housed, before it was installed on the southern edge of Westminster Bridge in 1902.

Another resident in the early 1900s was the great figure of English theatre, the actor-manager Sir Herbert Beerbohm Tree (1853–1917). In 1904 he established what became the Royal Academy of Dramatic Art (RADA), one of London's top drama schools today. He is particularly remembered and renowned for reintroducing and staging Shakespeare in the theatre.

Stations: Turnham Green and Stamford Brook

8. Zoffany House, No. 65 Strand on the Green

This striking three-storey brown- and red-brick house stands out on the Strand on account of its beautiful symmetry and architectural details. Dating from around 1704, it is typical of grand houses of the period with sash windows, an iron gate and railings and attractive Roman Doric pilasters surrounding the doorway. It is embellished by a pretty fanlight above the entrance and a climbing wisteria plant

Zoffany House. (© A. McMurdo)

that is particularly splendid in springtime. Home in the late 1700s to the German-born artist Johann Zoffany (1733–1810), the house today is designated by English Heritage as a Grade II* listed building both for its architectural and historic merits.

On his arrival in London in 1760 Zoffany worked for a clockmaker, painting scenes for clock faces. He went to live in Covent Garden, London's artistic hub at the time, and soon established a reputation for his portraits and theatrical 'history' paintings. He was both an excellent networker and a talented artist, and his informal style became very fashionable at a time when the well-to-do commissioned paintings to flaunt their wealth. Zoffany's work was quickly recognised by the leading actor-manager of the day, David Garrick, who became his first major patron. Subsequently the artist received the patronage of George III and his German wife, Charlotte, and with their support became a founding member of the Royal Academy. In a fairly short space of time Zoffany's fortunes had improved greatly, enabling him to move to the affluent Strand on the Green. However, his extravagant lifestyle meant he was forced to work abroad, first in Florence and later in India, in order to put his finances in order.

In 1789 he returned to Chiswick where he remained for the rest of his life, being buried in St Anne's Church, Kew Green. Since his death Zoffany House has changed hands many times. In the 1930s it was the home of Philip Hepworth, Principal Architect to the Commonwealth Commission, and in recent years to writer Carla Lane, to theatrical producer Tom Treadwell, and to animal activist Lord Chewton.

Stations: Kew Bridge, Chiswick and Gunnersbury

9. Hogarth House, Hogarth Lane

Thousands pass by William Hogarth's 'little country box', Hogarth House, every day as they drive along the A4 and cross Hogarth Roundabout, but are most probably unaware of its existence as it lies behind a wall at the busy intersection. Dating from around 1715, the attractive three-storey brick house with its oriel window and famous mulberry tree was originally constructed on land surrounded by fields and orchards. Located in the most idyllic position, it is a mere 4 miles from London and close to the River Thames. In 1749 artist William Hogarth (1697–1764) fell in love with the house and purchased it as a summer and weekend home. Many of Hogarth's friends and colleagues already had second homes in Chiswick and his decision to buy here demonstrated how successful he had become. Hogarth's reputation was mainly due to his satirical studies of eighteenth-century life, such as *Marriage a La Mode*, *Beer Street* and *Gin Lane*, where he highlighted the moral issues of the day. He mixed well with people from every class and background and was a great social observer.

Above: Hogarth House.
(© A. McMurdo)

Right: Hogarth House
Museum. (© A. McMurdo)

A gifted and prolific artist, he produced many engravings, prints and paintings throughout his career and in 1757 was appointed Sergeant-Painter to the King, greatly enhancing his status in society.

Although William and his wife Jane were childless, they welcomed children into their home; they invited youngsters from the Foundling Hospital in Bloomsbury (established by their friend, Thomas Coram) to stay with them in the summer, away from the noise and pollution of London. William was passionate about improving

Hogarth House Museum. (© A. McMurdo)

the lot of the many homeless children in London's streets and inspired by Coram's vision to deal with the problem he supported the work of the Foundling Hospital. He became a founder-governor and donated his own works to the charity.

Hogarth's impressive tomb is nearby in St Nicholas churchyard (q.v.) and today Hogarth House is a museum filled with displays of the artist's works and memorabilia. His much-loved garden has recently benefited from Heritage Lottery funding and has been beautifully restored much in line with its seventeenth-century origins.

Websites: www.wiiliamhogarthtrust.org.uk and www.hounslow.gov.uk

Stations: Turnham Green and Stamford Brook

10. Riverside Pubs: The City Barge and Bulls Head, Strand on the Green

These two well-loved pubs, sited either side of Kew Rail Bridge, have been a feature of the Strand for hundreds of years. Although the City Barge with its origins in the fifteenth century is the older of the two, it appears more modern as it was largely rebuilt after the Second World War. Today it operates as a gastro pub and offers wide-ranging menus based on fresh, seasonal ingredients. It is known for its fine

Above: The City Barge. (© A. McMurdo)

Below: Bulls Head. (© A. McMurdo)

wines and range of ales and has indoor and outdoor seating overlooking the river. Originally called the Navigator's Arms, its present name dates to 1807 when the City of London's state barge was regularly moored close by.

The Bulls Head dates to the 1700s and was first licensed in 1722. Over the years the pub acquired neighbouring cottages and is now a somewhat sprawling building. Inside, with its low ceilings and numerous nooks and crannies, the pub oozes with character. Like the City Barge it has a large outside terrace beside the river and is a popular venue. Despite assertions that a tunnel exists (once used by Oliver Cromwell) between the pub and Oliver's Eyot in the Thames, nothing has yet been found to corroborate this.

Stations: Kew Bridge, Chiswick and Gunnersbury

11. Chiswick House, Burlington Lane

When the 3rd Earl of Burlington, Richard Boyle (1694–1753), designed Chiswick House in the 1720s it was considered to be a revolutionary piece of architecture, a far move away from the baroque style of architects of the day. The villa, almost a perfect cube, fronted by two flights of stone stairs and an exquisite portico, is topped with an octagonal dome and eight unusual chimneys. It was largely modelled on the Italian architect Palladio's Villa Capra in Vicenza that had so moved the earl when he travelled to Italy in the early 1700s. Inspiration for the building also came from Inigo Jones and today you see statues of the two men on either side of the front portico.

The 'Architect Earl' was a rich aristocrat and a great patron of the arts. In contrast, his collaborator on the house and its grounds, William Kent (1685–1748), was a painter and architect from a humble Yorkshire background, and had become Burlington's protégé following their acquaintance in Italy.

Chiswick House. (© A. McMurdo)

Above: Chiswick House.
(© A. McMurdo)

Right: Chiswick House
Gardens. (© A. McMurdo)

Burlington drew up grand designs for his villa to include a magnificent octagonal room and long gallery on its upper floor and it is thought that Kent was involved in its interior decoration, especially the ceilings. In fact, the villa was not a home but a showpiece for Burlington's paintings, books and sculptures. During the earl's lifetime it was linked to a Jacobean house and this was where his guests would dine and be entertained.

After Burlington's death the house passed through marriage to the Dukes of Devonshire, who continued to provide lavish entertainment to the royals, politicians and celebrities of the day. The 6th Duke installed an exotic menagerie of kangaroos, giraffes and even an elephant and this was a great attraction for London society. Subsequently the house was tenanted to the Prince of Wales (the future Edward VII) and later sold to Middlesex County Council. After major restoration in the 1950s it was opened to the public.

Nowadays, it is administered by English Heritage and unsurprisingly has been the location for a number of films including *Harlots* (2017), *Vanity Fair* (2004) *and The Servant* (1963).

Websites: www.chisiwckhouseandgardens.org.uk and www.english-heritage.org.uk

Stations: Chiswick, Gunnersbury and Turnham Green

12. Chiswick House Gardens and Grounds

In the same way that Burlington's villa was considered to be a revolutionary design, his extensive gardens, landscaped by William Kent (1685–1748), were the talk of the town. They were laid out in a completely new style, largely modelled on gardens that would have existed in ancient Rome. Kent introduced ponds, cascades, greenery, and established sweeping lawns. In so doing he moved away from the conventional landscape designs of the day. His introduction of statues, ornamental buildings and beautiful vistas resulted in a much more informal layout. Kent envisaged the entire landscape as a picture and visitors

Ionic temple, Chiswick House Gardens. (© A. McMurdo)

Above: Classic bridge,
Chiswick House Gardens.
(© A. McMurdo)

Right: Serpentine Lake,
Chiswick House Gardens.
(© A. McMurdo)

experience this now when strolling around the grounds. You discover not only an avenue of sphinxes and urns, Roman statues, two obelisks, a Doric column, and a glorious bridge and cascade but also Kent's Ionic temple, situated beside a pool and facing a sunken amphitheatre. The gardens are enhanced all the more by the Inigo Jones Gateway, a gift to Burlington from Sir Hans Sloane. In the nineteenth century there were further additions made in the grounds by the 6th Duke of Devonshire. An enormous conservatory, 302 feet (96 metres) long, was designed by Samuel Ware and completed in 1813. It was the prototype for a number of glasshouses built around the country and the forerunner of London's Crystal Palace erected for the Great Exhibition in 1851. Today the conservatory is particularly renowned for its beautiful range of camellias on display each March. The collection contains many rare plants that are descended from the original 1828 planting and includes one of only two Middlemist's red camellias in the world, which arrived from China at the beginning of the 1800s with John Middlemist, a west London nurseryman. A delightful nineteenth-century Italian garden sits in a semicircle in front of Ware's conservatory, and a little beyond this is the Walled Garden, which was incorporated into the estate in 1812.

Chiswick House gardens have been a wonderful inspiration to gardeners for generations and nowadays are considered to be the birthplace of the English landscape movement and undoubtedly a testament to Kent's great talent.

Stations: Chiswick, and Gunnersbury and Turnham Green

13. Hammersmith Terrace

Hammersmith Terrace has long been associated with those connected to the Arts and Crafts movement. It is a terrace of seventeen listed Grade II houses dating from the 1750s and runs beside the River Thames. Unusually the gardens and

Hammersmith Terrace from the South Bank. (© A. McMurdo)

Hammersmith
Terrace.
(© A. McMurdo)

main rooms overlook the water and this side of the terrace displays features more commonly found on the front façade of Georgian terraced houses, such as the first-floor piano nobile and symmetrical windows. As a consequence of its design the street-facing side of Hammersmith Terrace is perhaps less visually pleasing, although its striking Doric porchways give it a character of its own.

No. 7, now a Grade II* listed building, became the family home from 1903 to 1933 of Sir Emery Walker (1851–1933), master printer, typographer, publisher and owner of Doves Press. Walker was great friends with William Morris (1834–96), the socialist activist and designer of fabrics, wallpaper and furniture. The two met daily to discuss politics and social issues and when Morris decided to set up his own Kelmscott Press, Walker acted as his advisor. Today, momentoes of their friendship are on display within No. 7 Hammersmith Terrace, which is now open to the public as a museum and offers tours on two days a week (see www.emerywalker.org.uk).

The building itself is a wonderful example of an Arts and Crafts house and has been kept as it was when Walker lived here, mainly due to the efforts of Elizabeth de Haas, his daughter Dorothy's companion, who later inherited the house.

No. 3 was home from 1905 to 1912 to Edward Johnston CBE (1872–1944). A remarkably talented calligrapher Johnston taught lettering and illumination at the Central School of Arts and Crafts. One of his students was sculptor and engraver Eric Gill, to whom he was a great inspiration. In the early twentieth century Johnston was commissioned by Frank Pick at London Underground to produce a new distinctive typeface and round logo for the company. Johnston's design, a clear and simple sans-serif typeface, was used by London Underground for the next sixty years and displayed on all its signs, posters and station nameboards.

Station: Stamford Brook

14. Riverside Buildings, Strand on the Green

On account of their proximity to the tidal River Thames many of the cottages, houses and buildings that border the river path have historically been liable to flooding especially at spring tides. With a tidal range of up to 7 meters (23 feet), the change in water level is enormous. The river flows right beside the path and houses so that when the tide is in it is wise not to walk too close to the edge! Likewise, when the tide has gone out a fall off the path could cause great injury as there is a drop of several meters to the mudflats below. Until the Thames Barrier was constructed in the early 1980s flooding here was much more common, and even though this rarely happens today there have been instances of the entire river path being submerged as witnessed in February 2016. Naturally, the history of flooding has encouraged residents to prepare for the eventuality, which explains why a number of the houses have built their front doors up high. You will pass by several properties that have added a small staircase leading up to their entrance while others have constructed wood, brick, metal or concrete barriers to prevent the water reaching their homes. Miniature doorways are both an unusual and interesting feature of the Strand.

From the late 1600s Strand on the Green had a thriving malting industry as Chiswick was renowned for its good quality barley. As many as five or six malthouses lined the riverside. Today, only one of the malthouses remains at No. 47 and has been converted into a house. It dates to the mid-nineteenth century and boasts prominent roof cowls that are seen best from the south bank of the Thames.

Another building of note is The Bell & Crown public house. Dating to 1907, it replaced an earlier eighteenth-century building and is a wonderful example of

Below left: Strand on the Green miniature doorways. (© A. McMurdo)

Below right: Strand on the Green miniature doorways. (© A. McMurdo)

Above: The Malt House. (© A. McMurdo)

Below: The Bell & Crown. (© A. McMurdo)

The Bell & Crown.
(© A. McMurdo)

Arts and Crafts design with its use of warm red brick, timber and metal windows. Today it is a popular pub noted both for its restaurant overlooking the water and for its excellent Fullers beers.

Stations: Kew Bridge, Chiswick and Turnham Green

15. George IV Public House, No. 185 Chiswick High Road

Despite being set back from the main high street the George IV pub is not easy to miss due to its prominent pub sign and welcoming exterior.

Today's building dates to the early 1930s but there has been a pub on this site since the 1770s when it was initially called Lord Boston's Arms. It acquired its present name around fifty years later around the time it was taken over by the local brewery Fuller, Smith & Turner, and it remains a pub in their portfolio today offering excellent food and ale. The pub, with its inviting dark wood-panelled interior, is much larger than it looks at first glance. There is a long bar area, glass partitions, a courtyard garden and several large function rooms upstairs. One of these, the Boston Room, is where the Headliners Comedy Club performs on Friday and Saturday nights and where jazz and quiz nights take place weekly. It is a great venue for parties and corporate hospitality and seats more than 200 guests.

The George IV pub is located on the road west from London that has always been a busy thoroughfare. Historically people travelled on horseback, later in horse and carts and then in stagecoaches, and from the early 1800s travellers came to the pub to buy a stagecoach ticket. Towards the end of the 1820s a new form of horse-drawn public transport, the omnibus, was introduced on to London's roads by George Shillibeer. It was considered revolutionary as it provided a regular service from Paddington to Bank for a set price of one shilling. Carrying twenty-two passengers in its covered vehicle, the omnibus would stop to

Above: The George IV. (© A. McMurdo)

Right: The George IV sign. (© A. McMurdo)

pick up and set down people all along the route. It became an instant success and unsurprisingly soon faced strong competition from other operators. One of these was George Cloud, who in 1838 ran a fleet of eight omnibuses from outside the George IV into London. The omnibus service grew so popular that ultimately there were too many vehicles vying for business, and it became quite common to see them racing one another for custom!

Stations: Chiswick Park and Turnham Green

16. Foster Books, No. 183 Chiswick High Road

This delightful bookstore is one of Chiswick's treasures and retains a loyal clientele. Based in the most attractive eighteenth-century building (said to be the oldest surviving shop on the High Road), Foster Books has been run by the same family for almost fifty years. The shop is full of character and reminiscent of the Dickensian era. Painted in racing green and with a prominent bow-fronted window, it stands out in the street.

Although independent bookshops are fairly rare in this day of the internet, Foster Books seems to have carved its own niche; the store stocks a great array of titles including children's and illustrated books, first editions, leather bound sets and fine bindings. Furthermore, the shop sells books about the local area, antique engravings and specialises in books that are difficult to find – maybe out of print or rare.

Foster Books.
(© A. McMurdo)

Foster Books has been selling books online for nearly twenty years through www.fosterbooks.co.uk but over the past decade it has diversified its activities by supplying books as props to the film and TV industries. Its books have thus appeared in movies such as *The Danish Girl* (2015) and *Mr Turner* (2014), as well as a number of *James Bond* movies and *Blade Runner 2049* (2017).

Stations: Chiswick Park and Turnham Green

17. The Lamb Brewery, off Church Street

Today all that is visibly left of Lamb Brewery is its high brick tower with the inscription bearing its name, easily seen from the Hogarth Roundabout. It stands close by the main Fullers, Smith & Turner brewery site and reminds us of the important part the brewing industry has played in Chiswick for hundreds of years. Both breweries claim to have started out their businesses in the eighteenth century from a brewhouse at Bedford House, Chiswick Mall, but there still remains a good deal of uncertainty about this. What is known is that in 1790 John Sich purchased the Lamb Brewery. He later formed a partnership with members of his own family producing beer but not selling it in public houses. When Sich retired from the business his partners diversified their interests into coal. This proved to be a wise move as it enabled the brewery to have its own much needed source of energy, and it was common to see Sich's barges transporting coal to the brewery premises. Throughout the 1800s heavy industry grew in Chiswick and there was a great increase in population, especially the working class. Unsurprisingly the heightened demand from this clientele increased Lamb Brewery's success, as well as the Sich family's affluence. The brewery continued to flourish and

Above: Lamb Brewery. (© A. McMurdo)

Below: Lamb Brewery. (© A. McMurdo)

many of the Sichs resided in Chiswick Mall's grand houses or in nearby Church Street. However, the brewing industry suffered a downturn in the late nineteenth and early twentieth century: recession struck, there were changes in the laws relating to licensing, and drinking hours were drastically reduced during and after the First World War, resulting in falling sales. By 1920 Lamb Brewery had closed down and was later sold to the Standard Yeast Company, who occupied the premises until 1952.

Today the brewery tower remains one of Chiswick's landmarks. The tower's beautiful dormer windows, ornamentation and ironwork stand proudly above the adjacent buildings. William Bradford, its architect, would no doubt be pleased to know it is still in use but probably be surprised to learn that it has now been converted into loft apartments.

Station: Turnham Green

18. Bedford House, The Avenue, Bedford Park

Designed by John Bedford, a local furniture maker and upholsterer, this was one of three houses to have been built here in 1793 and is the only one that still survives. It has undergone many changes over the past 200 years and is now converted into flats. Situated on the edge of The Avenue, one of Bedford Park's finest roads, it is faced in white stucco and exudes a sense of positive grandeur. It possesses some notable features, largely characterised by its tall chimneys,

Bedford House.
(© A. McMurdo)

its windows (including the very fine oriel window on its eastern side) and its stone gate piers. On the front of the house an English Heritage blue plaque remembers the botanist and horticulturalist John Lindley (1799–1865), who lived here from 1836 until his death. At that time there was a sizeable arboretum in the grounds and although this no longer exists, many of the trees were preserved when the Bedford Park estate was developed in the late nineteenth century.

Lindley came from Norfolk where his father owned a market garden. He moved to London in 1819 and was fortunate to find work in the herbarium of the leading botanist of the day, Sir Joseph Banks. Lindley's love of nature, gardens and botany led him to work for the Horticultural Society (now the Royal Horticultural Society) throughout much of his life. By the time he turned thirty he'd been appointed as the first Professor of Botany at University College London. He became an expert on orchids, identifying and naming a huge number of new varieties, which he included in his systematic classification of the species. This earned him the title 'Father of modern orchidology'. Despite his exceptionally busy life, lecturing to students and working as the secretary of the Horticultural Society, he found time to publish books on horticulture and botany and to edit *The Gardener's Chronicle* and *The Botanical Register.* Many consider his 1838 report on the future of the Royal Gardens at Kew to be his greatest achievement as this resulted in the gardens' preservation as a public scientific resource and the subsequent founding of the Royal Botanic Gardens, Kew.

Station: Turnham Green

19. Zachary House, No. 70 Strand on the Green

This is one of the Strand's most imposing houses and has been occupied by a number of public figures during the course of its lifetime. Today, it appears on the English Heritage register of listed houses, so any alterations that are carried out on the property have to adhere to strict regulations. Since the time it was built Zachary House has undergone a number of changes and is now characterised by its nineteenth century frontage and its pretty balconies. Most recently a further floor accommodating a fabulous roof terrace overlooking the river has been added as well as a large conservatory that connects the house to a mews cottage and cinema in the grounds.

The house gets its name from one of its first residents, a widow, Anna Maria Zachary. She lived here from 1797 and after her death it remained in the hands of her barrister son, Michael Mucklow Zachary, until the early 1820s. Towards the end of the century, noted local boatbuilder and architect William Sergeant (1836–1918) (q.v Grove Park Road) occupied the house, purchasing it in 1900

Zachary House. (© A. McMurdo)

and living here until 1917. Following his departure, the house became run down but was fortunately taken over and restored in the late 1920s by another architect, Sydney Clough, famous for his designs of Richmond Ice Rink. As a keen yachtsman the location of Zachary House was ideal for Clough and he became actively involved in the nearby Strand on the Green Sailing Club.

The first association that the house had with the music industry was in the 1960s when it featured in the Beatles' movie *A Hard Day's Night*, some of the scenes for which were filmed on the Strand. In the 1980s Zachary House was bought by Midge Ure, frontman of the rock band Ultravox. While living here he co-wrote the hit tune *Do They Know it's Christmas (Feed the World)* with Sir Bob Geldof, so heralding Zachary House as the birthplace of Band Aid. When Ure sold the house it then passed into the hands of Alan Smith, former editor of the *New Musical Express*.

Stations: Kew Bridge, Chiswick and Gunnersbury

2c. Fuller's Griffin Brewery, Great West Road, Chiswick Lane Mawson Arms; and the Fox & Hounds, Mawson Lane

The Fuller's Brewery is the oldest London brewery operating on its original site and also the largest brewery of its kind in the capital today. It has a history that stretches back over 300 years and is one of Chiswick's most valued local businesses, having been an integral part of the suburb's industrial success.

If you are interested in seeing the historic brewery buildings, learning about the beer-making process and perhaps sampling a beer or two, Fullers runs regular tours of its Griffin Brewery everyday except Sunday. For further details look at www.fullersbrewery.co.uk.

The earliest brewery was purchased by Thomas Mawson (1656–1714) in 1701 and remained in his family until 1782 when it was sold to John Thompson. On Thompson's death in 1807 his two sons took over control of the business that initially prospered, and in time became known as the Griffin Brewery. However, the sons started feuding and found themselves in financial difficulties. Their dire need for investment led them to forge a new partnership with an affluent country gentleman, John Fuller. When Fuller died in 1839 it was his son, John Bird Fuller, who turned the company around by bringing in new partners, two of whom, Henry Smith and John Turner, came from the Romford brewers Ind and Smith.

Griffin Brewery's main entrance. (© A. McMurdo)

Above: Griffin Brewery's shop. (© A. McMurdo)

Left: Griffin Brewery. (Asahi Europe)

The Mawson Arms and the Fox & Hounds. (© A. McMurdo)

Fuller, Smith & Turner came into existence in 1845 and descendants of the families still run the company today, although they are now involved wholly in their thriving hotel and pub portfolio. In 2019 they sold the Griffin Brewery to Japanese firm Asahi, who agreed to keep both the Fuller's brand and brewery.

As you would expect there are many Fuller's pubs in and around Chiswick but the most unusual has to be the one just around the corner from the Griffin Brewery. Bearing two names and displaying two different signs, it is hard to know whether it is called the Fox & Hounds or Mawson Arms. Indeed, for many years there had been two separate establishments here but in 1899 the two combined under the Mawson Arms banner, named in memory of the brewery's founder.

Station: Turnham Green

21. Christ Church, Turnham Green

In 1841 the vicar of St Nicholas in Church Street called a meeting to discuss the need for a new parish church in Chiswick. Up until this time all local parishioners attended St Nicholas beside the River Thames. The 1800s had, however, witnessed the development of much new industry in the area, which resulted in a huge surge in Chiswick's population, in particular around the Turnham Green area.

With agreement to begin the project monies were raised through public subscription and the Church Commissioners contributed the sum of £500, enabling the foundation stone of the new church to be laid in 1841.

The new Christ Church opened in 1843 and was built to the designs of William Bonython Moffatt (1812–87) and George Gilbert Scott (1811–78) in the Gothic Revival style. George Gilbert Scott subsequently set up his own business and went on to become one of the country's leading church architects of the Victorian age. Indeed, the church remains a wonderful example of his early work. In many respects, Scott can be compared to architects such as Norman Foster and Richard Rogers today – prolific and at the forefront of his profession. He has undoubtedly left his mark on numerous buildings throughout the country but for many his masterpiece has to be the Midland Grand Hotel above St Pancras station in London.

Christ Church stands out not only for its architectural style but also for its impressive flint exterior, red and black brick spire, its four-stage west tower and its elegant lancet windows. Today it bears an English Heritage Grade II listing largely on account of its design and location on the Green, but also in recognition

Christ Church. (© A. McMurdo)

Above left: Christ Church. (© A. McMurdo)

Above right: Christ Church. (© A. McMurdo)

of the care taken in subsequent alterations to the church maintaining its original character. Since its construction over 150 years ago it has seen a chancel added to the east end, the removal of its pews and the conversion of the west bays into two-storey community rooms. Much of the beautiful carved woodwork (screen, pulpit, stalls and panelling) within the building dates to 1906, the contribution of a talented group of craftswomen from the local polytechnic.

Stations: Chiswick Park and Turnham Green

22. British Grove Studios, No. 20 British Grove

These studios, owned by renowned musician and Dire Straits lead guitarist Mark Knopfler, are located in what was once the dye works of the Royal Laundry Chiswick. Both Chiswick and nearby Acton were renowned for these establishments during the late 1800s at a time when the suburbs were rapidly expanding and homes were being built for working-class families. In order to supplement the family income many of the women would take in washing, which was hard work, often done by hand. Laundries, varying in size from established

British Grove Studios. (© A. McMurdo)

businesses to small independent workers, served the local population, wealthy Londoners as well as major hotels. The Chiswick Royal Laundry consisted of a number of buildings and remained in business until the 1970s. After that time the dye works were used in a variety of ways including a wood workshop, warehouse, print room and even the record store and a small recording studio of Island Records (who occupied the main part of the laundry premises).

In the early 2000s Knopfler spent almost three years transforming the dye works into recording studios. Everything was rebuilt, and the walls and floor were surrounded by steel to avert background noise. The large and cavernous space was ideal, able to house the two British Grove Studios he was installing. It was his main aim to fill the studios with the very best vintage and new equipment. This is in clear evidence today with two rare old EMI mixing consoles (one on which the album *Band on the Run* was recorded) alongside the most state-of-the-art digital technology.

This has led to the studios achieving a spectacular client list including, among others, Razorlight, Adele, U2, Jamie Cullum, Sting, Ronan Keatin, Eric Clapton, Kasabian and The Rolling Stones. Although British Grove Studios have regularly been used to record Kopfler's own albums and film scores, it is available for commercial use too. So orchestral recordings and Hollywood blockbuster scores such as *Gravity* (2013), and *Mission Impossible: Rogue Nation* (2015) have all been recorded here. In 2009 the Music Producers Guild awarded Knopfler the 'Best Studio' award, confirming the success of his venture.

Station: Stamford Brook

23. The Steam Packet Public House, No. 85 Strand on the Green

This is one of Strand on the Green's most familiar buildings that until quite recently traded as a Café Rouge restaurant. Now, however, it has reverted to both its original name and function and is providing keen competition for the other pubs along the Strand. It is run by Food & Fuel, which has carefully restored the building, showing off its excellent Victorian features, especially the ornate ceilings and tiled walls. The company operates mainly in West London and manages several local pubs including The Roebuck (q.v.) on Chiswick High Road. The Steam Packet is known to have been licensed by 1870 and was listed in the 1881 census as 'Steam Packet Hotel At River Side'. The River Thames at this time was a busy working waterway filled with barges carrying provisions, fishing boats and wherries, as well as larger boats that belonged to the wealthy owners of the grand riverside houses. Steam packets first appeared on this part of the river in 1824 with the introduction of the Queenhithe to Twickenham service, from which the pub gets its name. The launches would dock at Kew Pier opposite the pub and it is still possible to walk down the flight of steps that lead from the road to the river, once used for loading and unloading the boats.

The Steam Packet.
(© A. McMurdo)

Above: The Steam Packet. (© A. McMurdo)

Below: The Steam Packet. (© A. McMurdo)

The packet trade was generally considered to be any scheduled cargo, mail or passenger service conducted by ship. In the early 1800s packet ships were characterised by the regularity of service, perhaps operating on a particular time or day of the week, a revolutionary step at the time. The word 'packet' in reference to a ship was first introduced in the sixteenth century and referred to mail that was transported on sailing ships between England and Ireland. Three centuries on they had been replaced by steamships and renamed steam packets.

The Steam Packet public house opens daily and prides itself on its range of local ales and seasonal food. Food is served both inside and outdoors, and upstairs there is a canopied terrace with splendid views across the river and Kew Bridge.

Stations: Kew Bridge, Chiswick and Gunnersbury

24. Bedford Park and No. 3 Blenheim Road

Work on Bedford Park began in 1875 and it was to become the first of its kind in the country, a forerunner to garden cities that developed during the twentieth century. It was the brainchild of cloth merchant Jonathan Carr (1845–1915), who was a speculator in property development and also had an interest in art. His vision was to build homes suitable for the middle classes, in the style of the Arts and Crafts movement, that so appreciated the craftsmanship in existence

House in Bedford Park. (© A. McMurdo)

Above left: House in Bedford Park. (© A. McMurdo)

Above right: No. 3 Blenheim Road. (© A. McMurdo)

before the time of mass industrialisation. Carr purchased land just close to the new Turnham Green station so that residents of Bedford Park would have easy access to work in London and yet live in a semi-rural location. He employed several architects to achieve his dream; the first was E. W. Godwin (1833–86), the actress Ellen Terry's lover, but he was quickly replaced by R. Norman Shaw (1831–1912) in 1877 and it is Shaw's legacy (and that of his assistant E. J. May) that largely remains today. Red-brick assymetric houses were built largely in the Queen Anne Revival style and adorned with hung tiles, terracotta decoration, balconies and gables, fronted with white-painted fences and surrounded by many mature trees. The new residents found the suburb aesthetically pleasing, especially as the houses were so markedly different to the stucco, classic and Gothic styles of earlier times. Bedford Park gained instant popularity and soon developed into a self-contained estate with a community centre, shops, church and public buildings.

Many of the houses were built with artist studios and this encouraged a number of artists and writers to move here. One of the latter was William Butler Yeats (1865–1939), the poet, playwright and Nobel Laureate, who moved to No. 3 Blenheim Road with his family in 1888. While living in Chiswick he made the acquaintance of personalities of the artistic world such as Oscar Wilde and William Morris and met the love of his life, Maud Gonne, who had a large influence over his writing. It was while living in Blenheim Road that Yeats composed his most celebrated poem, *The Lake Isle of Innisfree* (1890).

Station: Turnham Green

25. Former Chiswick Town Hall, Heathfield Terrace

This wonderful example of a Victorian civic building was built at a cost of £5,400 in 1876 and intended to house both the vestry's local government offices and provide meeting rooms for the local community. Designed in the Italianate style with stock brick and Bath stone dressings, the building is dominated by its grand porte-cochère entrance with its art nouveau ironwork. The work of J. Trahearne, the surveyor to the Chiswick Improvement Commissioners, the position of the building, set back from the road and facing leafy Turnham Green, certainly adds to its stature. Like Christ Church (q.v.) on Turnham Green, it acts as a focal point for the entire area. In the 1880s plans were drawn up for an extension that would cost a further £20,000. These were implemented and the building reopened in 1901 as the Town Hall of the newly established Chiswick District Council.

Chiswick Town Hall. (© A. McMurdo)

Above: Chiswick Town Hall. (© A. McMurdo)

Below: Chiswick Town Hall. (© A. McMurdo)

From its inception the Town Hall hired out its facilities and became a popular venue for concerts, balls, auctions, lectures and leisure classes. Functions of every type were held here including charity events, political meetings (the politician Mr Gladstone spoke here in 1880), and even ballet classes. The newly enlarged building now offered two halls, the larger with dressing rooms for the performers, as well as a council chamber and several meeting rooms. The interior décor was of the highest standard with stained glass, wood panelling, embossed tiling, oak and terrazzo floors and an imperial staircase with iron balustrades. It appears that the public spaces in Chiswick Town Hall were built to impress!

When Chiswick was incorporated into the borough of Hounslow in the 1960s its main services were transferred to the new borough council and the Town Hall building became largely redundant. Nowadays it houses offices and the local Citizens Advice Bureau but in keeping with its original heritage hires out many of its rooms. Dance, yoga, pilates and Zumba classes all take place here and it is where community and baby and toddler groups meet regularly. Unsurprisingly, the building is a popular wedding venue renowned for its range of settings and its lavish interiors.

Stations: Chiswick Park and Gunnersbury

26. London Buddhist Vihara – former Bedford Park Club – The Avenue, Bedford Park

This modest red-brick building was one of Bedford Park's earliest public buildings. Designed by R. Norman Shaw in 1877 as a club for the local residents, it is still a community hub but nowadays it is Theravada Buddhist monks who occupy the premises and hold regular services and classes here. The London Buddhist Vihara was established in Britain in 1926 by Anagarika Dharmapala, a Sri Lankan wanting to share the joys of Buddha's teachings with the English people, and the monastery moved here in the 1990s.

Before the Vihara's arrival the building had undergone much alteration, having been used as a social club for staff by CAV Ltd of Acton. The original club building was fitted out by William Morris, E. W. Godwin and William de Morgan in the Arts and Crafts style. Bedford Park Club was considered progressive for its time as it encouraged membership of both sexes. It was always extremely popular and frequented by many of the estate's artistic and bohemian residents. In its heyday the club offered its members numerous activities from dances, plays, lectures and masquerades to societies and a chess club, but sadly by 1939 its continued operation became uneconomic and it was forced to close.

Station: Turnham Green

London Buddhist Vihara. (© A. McMurdo)

27. Chiswick Park Station, Bollo Lane and Acton Lane

The design of Chiswick Park station is a superb example of the work of Charles Holden (1875–1960), an architect who made his mark on many of the War Graves Commission's cemeteries in France and Belgium, as well as on buildings and underground stations in the London area. Since 1987 the building has had Grade II listed status and remains largely unaltered from its original plan. It still boasts some wonderful original features such as its exterior drum, its signage, platform cantilevered canopies, an impressive tower, glazing and semicircular entrance hall.

Built on a difficult corner plot at the junction of two roads, the station is located in front of a curve on today's District Line. The present station, built in 1931–32, replaced an earlier one on the site, which was necessitated by the construction of two extra tracks to accommodate the Piccadilly Line (although the trains did not stop here). During the 1920s Holden had been working on a number of projects for the Underground Electric Railways Company of London (UERL). This included seven of the stations of its Northern Line extension to Morden, as well as the company's headquarters at No. 55 Broadway, now a Grade I listed building. From the moment UERL's managing director, Frank Pick, met Charles Holden he was greatly impressed by the architect's fine architectural designs and quality of work. Pick was committed to establishing a strong brand for the Underground and entrusted Holden with the commission to bring this about.

Above: Chiswick Park station.
(© A. McMurdo)

Right: Chiswick Park station.
(© A. McMurdo)

By the end of the 1930s the architect had designed fifty stations and his name, like Edward Johnston (q.v.), became very closely associated with the UERL. The contribution of both these talented men to the company's brand and style can still be seen all over London, making the stations instant recognisable landmarks.

Charles Holden was by all accounts a fairly modest man who was influenced by the writings of Walt Whitman. He declined the offer of a knighthood twice and believed in living simply.

Examples of his work can be seen at Senate House, London, and the former British Medical Association building on the Strand (now Zimbabwe House).

Station: Chiswick Park

28. Nos 68–74 Grove Park Road

Grove Park was the very first large Victorian housing estate to be built in Chiswick. Designed specifically for the affluent middle and upper classes, it is located in an ideal spot close to Strand on the Green between the river and the railway line. Its development came about due to the Duke of Devonshire, the landowner, who decided to build on the spacious grounds of his mansion, Grove House. Although work commenced in 1867, the estate took shape over several decades with many different developers involved in its formation. If you wander around its streets today you can still see the influence of the duke as many roads have names associated with his roots, his family, and his properties. For example, Hartington Road derives from the Marquis of Hartington, the title of the duke's eldest son, and Bolton Road is named after Bolton Abbey in Yorkshire, owned by the duke's family.

Nos 68–74 Grove Park Road are a group of four very large Gothic-style houses that back on to the Thames. They were built in 1874 by local architect William Sargeant (1836–1918), who lived nearby in Grove Park Terrace. The design was unusual for the time as Gothic architecture, with its turrets, stained glass and crow stepped gables, had largely gone out of fashion. Nonetheless, No. 70, known as Grove Mount, was home to actors John Thaw (1942-2002) and Sheila Hancock, his wife, between 1978 and 1998. Thaw is probably best known for his TV role as Inspector Morse, although he performed in numerous theatre, TV and film productions, ranging from Shakespeare to Captain Cook in Peter Pan. Sheila Hancock (b. 1933) still appears on radio programmes and in the theatre and has been equally prolific. Both actors have won many awards and Hancock received a CBE in 2011.

William Sargeant, who developed the houses here, also ran a successful boatbuilding business on the Strand. He is particularly celebrated for building the earliest boats powered by electricity and in 1888 for designing the *Viscountess Bury*, an eighty-seater electric passenger launch, the largest of its type in the world at the time.

Stations: Kew Bridge, Chiswick and Gunnersbury

Above: Grove Park Road houses.
(© A. McMurdo)

Right: Grove Park Road houses.
(© A. McMurdo)

29. Tabard Inn and Chiswick Playhouse, Bath Road

Just a moment away from Turnham Green underground station, the Tabard Inn was purposely constructed as a hotel, restaurant and pub for Bedford Park in 1880. Built in red brick, the Queen Anne-style pub is now a Grade II* listed building with a multitude of attractive external features. These include its unusual projecting first-floor bow windows, its tile-hanging tiled roofs and gables, and an entrance porch adorned with Tuscan columns. When it was constructed the pub was attached to Bedford Park's general stores. This was where residents came to shop not just for food but also for household goods, tools and even china, glass and ornaments. The General Stores also offered a post and telegraph office service so played a crucial role in the suburb. The stores survived until 1900 when they became an automobile works, and, later, office space.

The Tabard Inn was purposely designed not to emulate the large Victorian gin palaces that were so popular in the nineteenth century. These tended to be huge buildings, extravagantly fitted out with etched glass, ornate mirrors, long wooden bars, fancy ceilings and lit by gaslight. In contrast, R. Norman Shaw's plans for the pub were in keeping with Arts and Crafts philosophy, relying on good quality craftsmen such as William Crane and William de Morgan to produce the interior furnishings. Excellent examples of the tiles produced by both men can still be

The Tabard Inn and Chiswick Playhouse. (© A. McMurdo)

seen in the pub today along with other notable features such as the entrance lobby's glazed doors, chimneypieces and moulded dado rails.

Since 1985 the first floor of the Tabard has been used as a fringe theatre with a reputation for producing entertaining in-house plays and hosting those of other small theatre companies. Many established comedians have performed here including Al Murray, Russell Brand and Dara Ó Briain. In 2019 the theatre relaunched as the Chiswick Playhouse and has great hopes to reach a greater audience with its new ambitious programme.

Downstairs the pub, run by Greene King, serves a wide selection of beer and craft ales as well as food in its bars and in its beer garden.

Website: www.chiswickplayhouse.co.uk

Station: Turnham Green

30. St Michael and All Angels Church, Bath Road

Possibly the jewel of Bedford Park, the church is in the words of John Betjeman, 'a very fine example of R. Norman Shaw's work'. Located at the junction of Turnham Green Terrace and Bath Road and immediately opposite the Tabard Inn, St Michael's is undoubtedly a focal point of the area. Its classic red-brick exterior is in keeping

St Michael and All Angels Church. (© A. McMurdo)

Above left: St Michael and All Angels Church. (© A. McMurdo)

Above right: St Michael and All Angels Church. (© A. McMurdo)

with much of the housing in Bedford Park and complemented by white paintwork on timber balustrades above the ground-floor windows and on the porch gates. Shaw's building has many striking attributes, in particular the roof lantern with its glazed cupola and white balustrade and the church's beautiful west end window. Although St Michael's was consecrated in 1880, it was still far from complete, initially lacking a font, pulpit and reredos. In time, Maurice Adams, St Michael's first church warden and an assistant in Shaw's architectural practice, designed these church fixtures as well as a Gothic-style chapel and built the north aisle that had featured in Shaw's original plans for the church.

It is not just the façade of the church that has great appeal; the inside too is quite stunning and manages to combine two architectural styles: Gothic Perpendicular on the ground floor and Queen Anne Revival above. With its green painted interior woodwork, imposing columns, open roof and wide aisles, the church appears very spacious and is full of light.

Each year St Michael's runs the Bedford Park Festival and is also the venue of a literary festival in September. Now in its tenth year the Chiswick Book Festival attracts famous authors and readers and has been compared with Hay-on-Wye's literary festival. Throughout its history the borough has been a magnet for writers and many novelists, playwrights and poets, including in their number W. B. Yeats, Harold Pinter, John Osborne, Nancy Mitford and W. M. Thackeray have lived or worked here.

St Michael's is a church in the Anglo-Catholic tradition that acts as a hub for the local community. It not only hosts a range of classes in the parish hall but also holds regular musical concerts within the church itself.

Station: Turnham Green

31. St Nicholas Church, Church Street

St Nicholas was Chiswick's only parish church until 1843 when Christ Church (q.v.) was erected on Turnham Green. Actually, a church has existed on this site for at least 1,000 years, although the present building, with the exception of its fifteenth century tower, is relatively new, dating to the 1880s. It certainly seems fitting that the church is dedicated to St Nicholas, the patron saint of fishermen and sailors, as Chiswick's main industry for centuries was fishing, boatbuilding and riverside trades.

Today's church was designed by one of the Victorian period's most acclaimed ecclesiastical architects, James Loughborough Pearson (1817–97), famous in particular for his work at Truro Cathedral and Westminster Abbey. When planning the new church Pearson had to take into account the position of the site, between the medieval church tower (perhaps the oldest structure in Chiswick) and Church Street, and this led him to build the church almost as wide as it is long. Loughborough's church is built in the Perpendicular, Gothic Revival style and with its wood-beamed roof and large-stained windows, there is a distinct feeling of space inside. In fact, it seems much larger within than one expects from its exterior. Although the local landowner, the Duke of Devonshire, made a donation of £1,000 towards the project, nearly all the cost of the rebuilding was borne by Henry Smith, the industrious local brewer.

One of the most striking monuments within the church is in the Lady Chapel. Made of alabaster, it depicts the figures of Sir Thomas Chaloner (1561–1615) and his wife kneeling and facing each other across a prayer desk, beneath a Doric canopy with curtains held back by two soldiers. Sir Thomas Chaloner was a courtier in the time of Elizabeth I, a learned man and soldier, who also served as

St Nicholas
Church.
(© A. McMurdo)

Above: St Nicholas Church. (Thomas Faulkner)

Below: St Nicholas Church. (© A. McMurdo)

chamberlain to King James I's son, Henry, Prince of Wales. The church contains many other monuments, memorials and vaults including that of Lord Burlington.

St Nicholas has always been a fashionable wedding venue and in 1927 it was where the war hero Field Marshal Montgomery, 1st Viscount of Alamein, exchanged marriage vows with Betty Carver.

Station: Turnham Green

32. St Nicholas Churchyard and Burial Ground

For many years the churchyard was Chiswick's only burial ground and by the mid-1800s it was completely full and forced to close. Fortunately, a gift of much-needed land from the Duke of Devonshire allowed the churchyard to be enlarged and enabled it to reopen.

Surrounded by high walls, it is home to many impressive tombs and monuments. The most famous of these belongs to the eighteenth-century engraver, artist and caricaturist William Hogarth (1697–1764), who lived nearby in Hogarth House (q.v.). His body and that of several members of his family are buried under a monument capped by an urn and bearing an epitaph that begins with the line, 'Farewell, great painter of mankind'. It was written by Hogarth's friend and admirer, the actor-manager David Garrick. Nearby, beneath a fine table tomb, said to be the work of the architect William Kent (1685–1748), lies Richard Wright,

Above: Foscolo's Tomb, St Nicholas churchyard. (© A. McMurdo)

Right: Hogarth's tomb, St Nicholas churchyard. (© A. McMurdo)

who was Lord Burlington's builder and bricklayer. The remains of Kent himself are said to be interred within the Burlington family vault.

There are many other tombs and graves of famous people within the churchyard including the founder of Bedford Park, Jonathan Carr (1845–1915), Charles II's mistress Barbara Villiers (1640–1709), and Henry Joy (d. 1893), who sounded the 'Charge of the Light Brigade'. American-born painter James Abbott McNeill Whistler (1834–1903) is buried in the western part of the graveyard under a fine bronze sarcophagus. From the age of twenty-five Whistler spent much of his working life in London and became renowned for his night scenes of the River Thames, known as 'nocturnes'. A short distance away is the tomb of Strasbourg-born painter P. J. de Loutherbourg (1740–1812), designed by the architect Sir John Soane. Loutherbourg was particularly known for his intricate set designs for London theatres and for his large naval paintings, some of which now form part of the Royal Museums Greenwich collection. Nearby, surrounded by railings, is the impressive tomb of Italian patriot and poet Ugo Foscolo (1778–1827). Although initially buried here, Foscolo's remains were later exhumed and returned to Florence at the request of the King of Italy.

Station: Turnham Green

33. Said House, Chiswick Mall

Said House has the perfect riverside location on Chiswick Mall and is easily recognised for its prominent, curved glass window above the garage, its ornamental urns and stone lions and its imposing entrance accessed by two flights of stairs. It is a large five-bed property that boasts a billiard room, roof terrace and a housekeeper's annexe and has two attractive gardens, one separated from the main body of the house beside the Thames, the other at the rear of the house. Although parts of the building date to Georgian times, the house has undergone a number of alterations during the course of its existence.

In the early 1930s it became the home of highly acclaimed actor-manager Sir Nigel Playfair (1874–1934), and it was he who installed the west extension to Said House. Playfair, who was educated at Harrow and Oxford, began a career in law but later decided to turn his hand to acting and the theatre. Throughout his career he was associated with the Lyric Theatre in Hammersmith and was applauded for many of his slightly unconventional productions there. He is particularly noted for having brought Shakespeare into the modern age with his production of 'As You Like It' in 1920. Playfair was also greatly involved with the BBC and commissioned the first radio play on English radio but it was for his contribution to the theatre that he was awarded a knighthood in 1928.

Said House itself rose to instant fame in 2005 when it was seen by millions watching the first series of *The Apprentice* on UK television. Five years earlier when *Big Brother* hit the screens it paved the way for a programme of this type

Said House. (© A. McMurdo)

and so it was no surprise that the new reality TV series immediately drew such a large and loyal audience. Filming took place at the house in the spring of 2005 and viewers soon became familiar with its interior spaces and exterior façade during the weekly episodes when contestants vied with one another to reach the ultimate prize of becoming the apprentice to the successful entrepreneur Sir Alan Sugar.

Station: Turnham Green

34. High Road House, Nos 162–170 Chiswick High Road

This five-storey building, occupying a corner plot between Turnham Green Terrace and Chiswick High Road, is very well situated as Turnham Green underground station is only a few moments away and it sits on the main route into central London. Built around the late 1800s, it is made up of a row of four terraced houses still bearing many original architectural details. Nowadays it operates as High Road House, a private members club and chic boutique hotel and is part of the international Soho House group.

High Road House. (© A. McMurdo)

For over twenty years the premises was home to Foubert's Hotel, run by the Lodico family. When the family put it on the market in the early 2000s it was rumoured that local personalities Ant and Dec were planning an £8 million bid for it. However, their plans didn't materialise, and Soho House was able to go ahead with the purchase, adding the hotel to its ever-growing portfolio.

High Road House today mainly operates as a private members club for those working in the creative industries. Members of the public can dine at its excellent ground-floor brasserie and outdoor terrace while club members have access to the upstairs lounge, restaurant and bar and to the fashionably designed hotel bedrooms.

Station: Turnham Green

35. The Old Cinema, No. 160 Chiswick High Road

As its name suggests this building, right next to High Road House, was once a cinema. It started life in 1888 when, as Chiswick Hall, it was licensed as a centre for music and dancing. Many social and demographic changes were taking place around this time: Chiswick's population was growing significantly and as the Victorian age was nearing its end local residents were looking for more than just traditional entertainments. Moving images had gradually appeared at sites around the country, often viewed in shops or at fairground shows, which attracted hordes of people and made lots of money for their promoters As the popularity of the moving picture industry grew and entrepreneurs realised how lucrative this modern and fashionable entertainment could be they started to build permanent cinemas. In Chiswick the first cinemas appeared in 1909, and three years later the Cinema Royal, a sizeable building that could accommodate 450 people, opened its doors at No. 160 Chiswick High Road. The majority of films screened at the time came from America and Chiswick's cinemas were always in competition with one another to attract the greatest audience numbers. Competition was so fierce that for a three-month period in 1925 the Royal shut down. It recovered for a while and went on to introduce sound before finally shutting its doors in 1933. Following its closure the building was briefly used for parachute storage before reopening as a shop selling traditional British antiques to overseas buyers (in great demand at the time).

From the early 1970s the premises took on a new persona as 'The Old Cinema' and established a store selling retro and vintage antiques. Since that time its product range has expanded dramatically and has become increasingly eclectic. The showrooms stock everything from industrial and domestic furniture, decorative objects, lighting, jewellery, fashion and textiles and much more. It is in every sense a real Aladdin's cave and an absolute delight to visit. There is no doubt that for anyone fitting out a restaurant, bar, shop, home or needing props for a movie this should be their first port of call!

Station: Turnham Green

Above: The Old Cinema. (© A. McMurdo)

Right: The Old Cinema. (© A. McMurdo)

The Old Cinema. (© A. McMurdo)

36. Chiswick Public Library, No. 1 Duke's Avenue

In 1890 a modest house on the corner of Duke Road and Bourne Place was opened as Chiswick's first public library. It received instant acclaim and was hailed as a great asset for the local community. Ever since the Public Libraries Bill had been enacted in 1850 new libraries had sprung up all over the country and free books were now available to many in the population, often for the first time. Chiswick's public library was a success from the start and despite the long opening hours (from 09.00 to 22.00 on most weekdays), the building was always thronged with people. Unlike today readers could only borrow one book at a time and they had no access to the bookshelves. They had to choose the title they wanted from a catalogue and it would be delivered to them by the librarian or an assistant. The lending library was located on the first floor and borrowers frequently queued on the stairs to take out or return their books. Such overcrowding was certainly inconvenient and uncomfortable but even worse was the unhealthy environment caused by the gas lighting within the library's rooms. It was obvious to its users that a new home was needed for the service, but the council had failed to find an alternative site, mainly because of difficulties with funding. Several plans were put forward by the council's subcommittee, but nothing came of any of them and the need to move became ever more pressing.

Chiswick Public Library. (© A. McMurdo)

Quite unexpectedly the problem was solved in 1897 when local businessman and wallpaper manufacturer Arthur Sanderson (q.v.) philanthropically gifted his family home at No. 1 Duke's Avenue to the council for use as a library. He stated the Queen's Golden Jubilee to be his motivation, thinking that it would be a 'fitting' way of celebrating the occasion. The council was delighted with Sanderson's bequest and work quickly began on converting the very attractive substantial three-storey house into suitable library premises, where it remains to this day. It is unquestionably one of Chiswick's landmark buildings and continues to play a leading and vital role in the local community.

Stations: Chiswick Park and Turnham Green

37. The Fire Station, No. 197 Chiswick High Road

Today No. 197 Chiswick Fire Station is a popular neighbourhood bar and restaurant occupying the site of Chiswick's first fire station. When the station was built in 1891 its tall tower was the earliest of its type in London, erected as a place to dry the firemen's hoses. This was not the station's only unusual feature as it housed a mortuary where many of the firemen would work to increase their

Above: 197 Chiswick Fire Station. (© A. McMurdo)

Left: 197 Chiswick Fire Station. (© A. McMurdo)

income and had its own stables where the horses used to pull the early fire engines were housed. By 1936 the force and its apparatus had outgrown the premises so was forced to leave No. 197 Chiswick High Road. It wasn't until the 1960s that a new permanent base was established for the Fire Service in nearby Heathfield Gardens.

Chiswick's Victorian fire station is certainly a marvellous example of the work of the London County Council's fire brigade department, which, inspired by the Arts and Crafts movement, was renowned for designing buildings to the highest specification. The warm red-brick and stone exterior, large windows and decorative curved gables are in keeping with much of Chiswick's domestic buildings and demonstrate how a well-designed civic building can contribute to the character of the local area.

Stations: Turnham Green and Chiswick Park

38. The Crown Public House, No. 210 Chiswick High Road

The Crown, like so many buildings in Chiswick, had an entirely different purpose when it opened in the last decade of the nineteenth century. There are few clues to identify what went on here initially, but its prominent crest above the main entrance surely indicates that it was a building of importance. In fact, it was the home of Chiswick's first purpose-built police station, which operated here for eighty years before transferring across the street in 1972.

No formal centralised police service existed in the country until 1829 when the Home Secretary, Robert Peel, introduced a bill in Parliament that led to

Above: The Crown.
(© A. McMurdo)

Right: The Crown.
(© A. McMurdo)

the formation of his famous Metropolitan Police Force. The officers, known as 'bobbies' were easily recognised by their smart uniforms, top hats, and truncheons. Until this time, policing was largely unorganised and often carried out on a voluntary basis, directed at catching villains as opposed to undertaking criminal investigation. It was considered the duty of every citizen to arrest those breaking the law and to attract the attention of passers-by or the parish constable. Chiswick had already set up its own subscriber law-enforcing service in 1798 to help protect its residents and their property, with fees being placed in a fund to cover the costs of prosecution and to publicise rewards. Once the Metropolitan Police Force was established Chiswick gained its own sergeant and constables, and by the late 1800s the police station employed seventy-three policemen dealing with anything from major crimes to drunken brawls. Those arrested would be detained in the station's cells.

Today, one of these cells, The Nook, is a comfy space used for wining and dining in The Crown, but no other evidence of the building's former usage is evident. It is a modern and stylish venue where food created by the Sicilian chef is served all day, available both at the bar or in one of The Crown's dining rooms or in the courtyard garden. There is also an art deco bar serving a wide range of cocktails and selection of keg beers and fine wines.

Stations: Turnham Green and Chiswick Park

39. Ancient Inns, Chiswick High Road

That Chiswick is home to numerous inns and bars is not surprising. Built on the main highway west from London, it has always been an area where travellers would stop to eat, drink or perhaps to rest before continuing their journeys. Stagecoaches would use the facilities at the coaching inns to care and feed their horses or to find a fresh team and the inns thus became an essential part of the transport infrastructure. Over the years some of the inns have been rebuilt (especially during the Victorian age), some have completely disappeared, but many still remain bearing the name they have had for several centuries.

The Roebuck is one such inn and has been licensed at No. 122 Chiswick High Road for almost 300 years. The pub was completely rebuilt in 1893 when its large stables and bowling green were replaced by the terrace of shops and housing attached to it today. Over the years it has changed its name several times but has since reverted to The Roebuck and the building now sports an eye-catching relief of a large deer on its roof gable. The pub is run by the Food & Fuel group and offers top-quality cuisine and a wide range of beers, wines and gins in its comfortable bar and dining room.

A few hundred metres west along the High Road brings you to the Old Pack Horse. Located at No. 434 Chiswick High Road, it is sited on the corner of Acton Lane and Chiswick High Road. The pub has existed here since the seventeenth century and in 1808 was acquired by local brewers Fuller, Smith & Turner. In 1905 it was rebuilt in red brick and stone with terracotta and enhanced by wonderful decorative Corinthian pillars, mullion windows, balustrades, and colourful decorative tiling. Its design and ornamentation, the work of the brewery's

Above left: The Roebuck. (© A. McMurdo)

Above right: The Old Packhorse. (© A. McMurdo)

Below: The Old Packhorse. (© A. McMurdo)

house architect, Nowell Parr (1864–1933), has always been lauded, especially the pub's external façade. Its striking exterior continues to be a focal point of the Turnham Green area and, as in times gone by, attracts people from far and wide.

Stations: Turnham Green and Chiswick Park

40. Sanderson's and Barley Mow Passage

In 1879 Arthur Sanderson set up his wallpaper manufacturing factory in Chiswick on the site of what had once been a militia barracks. So successful was the business that by the end of the 1800s the firm had expanded into several new buildings in and around Barley Mow Passage. When Arthur died in 1882 the firm was taken over by his three sons, John, Arthur and Harold. The latter, who as a young man had been apprenticed at the Chiswick works, took over responsibility for the company's design, production and management. It was under his stewardship that the business prospered significantly, and Sanderson's reputation grew both at home and abroad. Although the company still produced printed wallpaper by hand, it had managed to hone its manufacturing processes to produce machine-made middle-range wallpapers in an economic way without stinting on quality. Sanderson's increasing commercial success made it one of Chiswick's most illustrious businesses and it was compelled to build another factory nearby in order to keep up with the ever-growing demand. By the early 1900s the firm's plant extended from Duke's Avenue and along Barley Mow Passage, employing almost a thousand employees.

In October 1928 the company was struck by a major fire in its older premises, causing enormous devastation to its plant, stock and buildings. Even though the management and staff worked hard to get the business back on track, the fire caused great damage to the company and within two years the entire plant in Chiswick closed down and Sanderson moved into new state-of-the-art premises in Perivale.

The old factory building was subsequently rebuilt and from 1976 became known as the Barley Mow Workshop. It was an entirely new concept for office premises in the UK, which was set up by two architects, David Rock and John Townsend. They envisaged commercial spaces that could be rented out by small businesses or industrial units paying their share on a pro rata basis for use of the Workshop's centralised facilities (such as secretarial, administration, reception and cleaning services). The architects' innovative idea has been copied many times since and is especially popular with start-ups and small businesses.

Tube stations: Chiswick Park and Turnham Green

Above: The Barley Mow Centre. (© A. McMurdo)

Below: The Barley Mow Centre. (© A. McMurdo)

41. The Voysey Building, Barley Mow Passage

Almost opposite the Barley Mow Workshop is the most unexpected white-tiled building with a prominent wavy roofline. Today, known as Voysey House, it is used as offices but was built in 1902–03 as a new extension to Sanderson's factory and linked to the works via a footbridge. Its architect, local Bedford Park resident C. F. A. Voysey (1857–1941), was a proponent of the Arts and Crafts movement and took inspiration from William Morris.

Sanderson's commissioned Voysey first to produce wallpaper for the company, and later, furniture for their social club on Chiswick High Road. The new factory block, providing space for printing machines and the block and roller cutting and stencilling departments, was acclaimed as a 'model factory with a feeling of airiness and spaciousness'. Its overall design certainly demonstrates Voysey's focus on form and function rather than decoration and is a wonderful example of an Arts and Craft factory building, now Grade II* listed. Interestingly, this was his only venture into industrial architecture, and he is best remembered for his domestic buildings such as No. 14 South Parade, Bedford Park. Built in white stucco as an artist's cottage, Voysey specifically designed it to stand apart from what he considered as the bland red-brick housing of the suburb.

Stations: Chiswick Park and Turnham Green

The Voysey Building. (© A. McMurdo)

Voysey House, South Parade. (© A. McMurdo)

42. Harold Pinter's Home, No. 373 Chiswick High Road

No. 373 Chiswick High Road is a tall, fine brick, four-storey semi-detached house that was built in the late 1800s. It is a substantial building characterised by its white stone quoins, pitched roof, bow windows and decorated gables. Here in the late 1950s the Nobel Prize winner Harold Pinter (1930–2008) wrote his play *The Caretaker*. The play was initially staged at the small arts theatre in Piccadilly but was such an astounding success (there were twelve curtain calls on its opening night) that it immediately transferred to London's Duchess Theatre and ran for 444 performances. The original cast included Donald Pleasance and Alan Bates and won the *Evening Standard* award for Best Play 1960.

The Caretaker proved to be the turning-point in Pinter's career, making him instantly famous, wealthier and provided the security he sought. This play was in many ways typical of Pinter's writing: full of long pauses, lacking in action, set in squalid conditions and quite repetitive. Audiences were spellbound by its message and seemed not to mind that the author expected them to form their own opinions as to the play's outcome.

Pinter's inspiration for the play came from his own real-life experience. He and his actor wife, Vivien Merchant, and their newborn son had moved into the tiny first-floor Chiswick flat in 1958 when Pinter was making a living taking acting roles and BBC commissions for radio plays. They shared the house with its owner, a builder, who was absent more often than he was there and the builder's brother,

Pinter's lodgings. (© A. McMurdo)

an introverted character, who had a history of mental health problems. One day the brother brought a tramp home who stayed in the house for several weeks. Pinter was motivated to write *The Caretaker* from observing how the men interacted, and his characters, Mick and Aston, are based on the two brothers, while Davies represents the tramp. Recounting the story of the three men who find themselves in a power struggle *The Caretaker* is the play that finally cemented Pinter's reputation and today is still one of the best-known of the thirty-two plays he wrote.

Stations: Gunnersbury and Chiswick Park

43. Former Tram Depot and Power House, Nos 70–72 Chiswick High Road

When you turn off Chiswick High Road and see the Stamford Brook Bus Garage and Power House it seems hard to imagine that this was an area of orchards and gardens until the late nineteenth century. The site was initially purchased by the local Tram Railway Company to build a three-track shed and stables for their horse-drawn tram service, but when an electric tram service was introduced in the late 1890s (the first in London), the site was rebuilt by London United Tramways (LUT) as a depot for the new electric trams and as their headquarters.

Alongside the depot the LUT had a large power station erected to provide the trams with the power they required. It was, according to the architectural historian Nicholas Pevsner, the most exciting building in the area, and many still regard it so today. Built in red brick and stone, it is an enormous flamboyant baroque structure that flaunts two enormous carved figures above the entrance representing 'electricity' and 'locomotion'. Architects William Curtis Green and J. Clifton Robinson created a magnificent building at the forefront of engineering technology that stayed in use until 1962 but was then left unused and largely neglected. Thankfully, Metropolis recording studios discovered the building in the 1980s, decided to restore it to its former glory and to convert its wonderful spaces for their recording suites and to construct flats in the roof area. The interior now boasts a stunning 20-metre-high atrium filled with platforms and walkways, and even one of the building's original ornate iron staircases. Metropolis Studios are today renowned worldwide for their studios and their A-list client list (including, among others, Queen, Jay-Z, Amy Winehouse, Prince and Rihanna).

The tram depot next door has had a slightly chequered history but always in connection with buses and transport. It was reopened as Stamford Bridge bus station in 1980 after a £2 million refit when great care was taken to restore its façade. Although much plainer than the Power House, it has distinctive features including an imposing pediment surmounted by a central clock and complements its neighbouring building.

Stations: Turnham Green and Stamford Brook

VIEW OF CENTRAL POWER HOUSE AND CAR SHEDS ON OPENING DAY.

Central Power House and car sheds on opening day. (Courtesy of Hounslow Archives & Local Studies Centre)

Former car sheds, Stamford Brook Bus Depot. (© A. McMurdo)

44. Former Army and Navy Furniture Depository, Heathfield Terrace

Like the Power House (q.v.), this is another Chiswick building that has changed usage in recent times. In 1988, around a century after it opened as a furniture depository for the Army and Navy stores, it was converted into a block of flats and renamed No. 9 Devonhurst Place. Located close to the Barley Mow former Sanderson (q.v.) factories, it has an ideal position facing the large leafy expanse of Turnham Green and maintains a definite presence in the area. It is a massive building enhanced by its warm red-brick exterior, its many windows (circular at penthouse level) and a classic central pediment. The present-day flats are widely sought after for their character as well as their position right by Chiswick High Road, its shops and transport.

A much lower building, only one storey high, stands immediately in front of the flats. Dating to 1891, it boasts an unusual wooden cantilevered roof and was once used as an auction room for the Army and Navy Stores, but in recent times it has been the home of a music company.

The Army and Navy Co-Operative Society was formed in 1871 by a group of army and naval officers keen to make domestic goods available to its members at the lowest prices. Originally it was a member-only service – perhaps comparable to Amazon Prime today. Membership was open to serving, non-commissioned and petty officers, those connected with military organisations or part of a

Above: Former Army and
Navy Furniture Depository.
(© A. McMurdo)

Right: Former Army and
Navy Furniture Depository.
(© A. McMurdo)

military family, and widows of officers. Members benefited from profit share and free delivery of their purchases and the Co-Operative operated rather like a club, thriving in the days of the Empire.

In 1872 a shop was opened in Victoria Street initially selling just groceries, but the range of goods was soon extended and members (and later civilians too) were able to purchase drapery, stationery, clothing and fancy goods. By the mid-1880s the Co-Operative had its own estate agency, banking department and was selling furniture. The latter became rapidly popular and led to the need for a storage facility, which the Army and Navy Stores found at the Sanderson's site on Heathfield Terrace.

Stations: Chiswick Park and Turnham Green

45. Our Lady of Grace and St Edward, No. 247 Chiswick High Road

An attractive red-tiled church serving Chiswick's small Catholic community was established here in the 1860s and dedicated to St Mary. Within twenty years the congregation had grown so greatly that St Mary's could no longer accommodate its members and was demolished to make way for a new much larger church, dedicated to Our Lady of Grace and St Edward. The influx of Catholics into the area, a result of horrific famine in Ireland in the 1840s, meant that many came to work in Chiswick's market gardens and set up home here. This new church, designed by Kelly and Birchall, was built in the Italian Renaissance style and consecrated in 1904. Although the original plans included a tower, it was not

Our Lady of Grace and St Edward Church. (© A. McMurdo)

Above: Our Lady of Grace and St Edward
Church. (© A. McMurdo)

Right: Our Lady of Grace and St Edward
Church. (© A. McMurdo)

built until 1930 and then as a memorial to parishioners killed during the First World War. Interestingly, its designer was Giles Gilbert Scott, the grandson of the eminent Victorian architect George Gilbert Scott, who had designed Christ Church, Turnham Green (q.v.).

The interior of the church, although fairly plain, is embellished by the chancel's wonderful marble furnishings and Corinthian columns. Outside, the church is characterised by its deep red brickwork, its campanile, and wonderful terracotta mouldings including a frieze of swags and winged cherub heads.

Stations: Chiswick Park and Turnham Green

46. Former Pier House Laundry, Nos 86–94 Strand on the Green

In its heyday the laundry was one of the largest in London and employed 200 staff. The premises would have been bustling with laundry hands, washers, dyers, ironers, labourers, packers and sorters, laundry girls and even carmen, waiting to deliver the laundry to one of its nineteen collection shops.

Pier House Laundry was established in 1860 by a French immigrant, Camille Simon, at a time of great growth in the laundry industry in West London. From the middle of the century laundry services, many of them small businesses operating in their own homes, vied for business in the Chiswick and Acton areas. In fact, there were so many laundries in nearby South Acton that it became known as Soapsud Island. Camille Simon's laundry was a substantial concern from the start. Under his, and later his son's, management it flourished and by 1905 the business was compelled to move out of the original buildings by the river next to Kew Bridge into a new much larger purpose-built laundry across the road in Strand on the Green. The business continued to thrive and so an extension was added in 1914. This was a period when there was an ever-increasing demand for cleaning services as more and more people moved away from central London into the suburbs. Custom came not just from individuals but from large houses in the area and organisations in London's West End, such as catering companies and hotels. It was unquestionably a boom time for the laundry industry, which lasted until the first laundrettes appeared in High Streets in post-war Britain.

Pier House Laundry was always a well-run family business. It remained prosperous until 1973 but then ceased trading due to difficulties in finding suitable staff. It was Camille's grandson, Leonard, who finally sold the business, and in the 1980s the laundry building was converted into office space, although its façade was retained as a reminder of its industrial heritage and significance. Pier House suffered a devastating fire in 2016 when much of its 1980s steel frame was damaged. It has just reopened following a major restoration and an extension project.

Stations: Kew Bridge and Gunnersbury

Above: Pier House Laundry. (Courtesy of Hounslow Archives & Local Studies Centre)

Below: Pier House today. (© A. McMurdo)

Pier House Laundry. (Courtesy of Hounslow Archives & Local Studies Centre)

Pier House Laundry. (Courtesy of Hounslow Archives & Local Studies Centre)

47. Chiswick Empire, Nos 414–424 Chiswick High Road

Today, a blue-windowed office block stands on the site of what for forty-seven years had been the Chiswick Empire, one of suburban London's most eminent entertainment venues. When the idea for a music hall was mooted in 1910 there had been vehement local opposition to building it in Chiswick as it was feared that such a venue would lower the tone of the area, but construction went ahead, and the theatre opened in 1912. It was the brainchild of impresario Sir Oswald Stoll (1866–1942), who engaged celebrated theatre architect Frank Matcham to design his theatre. The Chiswick Empire became an immediate success, and its stately neoclassical frontage facing Turnham Green and Christ Church, a local landmark. The interior of the theatre was plush, decorated in pale cream and old gold and complemented by bottle green upholstery. Seating nearly 2,000, it had an orchestra pit that accommodated fifteen musicians and there were ten dressing rooms for the artistes. Many stars appeared here in the Empire's music hall entertainment, plays, revues, variety shows and even opera and ballet, and the annual pantomime was always a huge draw. Before the First World War, the Empire attracted big names such as Sybil Thorndyke and George Formby, and in the 1940s and 1950s it was where Vera Lynn, Laurel and Hardy, Terry Thomas and Arthur Askey all performed. It even became a cinema for a while in the 1930s but reverted to variety shortly after.

Empire House. (© A. McMurdo)

Empire Theatre poster. (Courtesy of Hounslow Archives & Local Studies Centre)

The theatre was always popular and played to packed audiences, night after night. So, when the staff were told in 1959 that the Empire was to shut down it came as a great surprise. The final performance at the Empire took place in June, with flamboyant American artiste Liberace playing to a full house, and it was reported that the theatre had 'died with dignity'. Within a month the building had been demolished and planning permission given for an eleven-storey office block, Empire House, to be built in its place. Empire House remains in situ today but is empty and waiting redevelopment, perhaps as an hotel or apartment block.

Station: Chiswick Park

48. Chiswick Quay

This small housing development of sixty-eight houses was created in the mid-1970s around an ornamental lake in the grounds of Grove House, once part of Lord Burlington's Chiswick House estate. Its architects, Bernard Engels and Partners, turned the lake into a marina, with access to the Thames via a lock, and built an estate of large mainly four-storey houses set out in terraces around the water, giving each house its own mooring space. The architects were largely influenced in their design by an avant-garde village development around water that had been conceived by French architect Francois Spoerry in Port Grimaud in 1966. They endeavoured to make an interesting layout for Chiswick Quay by introducing different roof heights and staggering the house frontages to make them less uniform. They also utilised different surface materials so that some of the houses were tile-hung while others were painted white. Each house was built facing water, either the marina or the River Thames, and as the terraces enclosed the marina on three sides, it made the area safe for boat owners. Not surprisingly Chiswick Quay's houses have always been highly priced and are quickly snapped up when put on the market.

In the early twentieth century the lake was used for pleasure purposes by the residents of Grove Park estate but during the First World War to aid the war effort, it was converted along with a Thames cutting for use as a dock. Here, concrete barges were constructed and then used to transport ammunition to France.

Interestingly, the lake had acquired the name Cubitt's Yacht Basin at some point in its history. No one is quite sure why but there is a legend that asserts that it was here that architect-builder Thomas Cubitt (1788–1855), responsible for building luxurious Pimlico and Belgravia, unloaded the fine Portland stone later used in their construction.

Chiswick Quay. (© A. McMurdo)

Chiswick Quay. (© A. McMurdo)

During the interwar years, the lake became home to a motor yacht club but was then supplanted by a colourful community of houseboats and artists who stayed here until driven out by the developers when work began on Chiswick Quay in the late 1960s.

Station: Chiswick

49. The Cathedral of the Nativity of the Most Holy Mother of God and the Royal Martyrs, No. 57 Harvard Road

The Russian Orthodox Cathedral, with its distinctive bright blue dome, gold stars and magnificent golden cross, is a real focal point in Chiswick that stands out like a beacon. In fact, many people are drawn to its onion dome as they travel on the A4/M4 to or from Heathrow Airport and beyond. The cathedral itself is relatively new to the district (it was built in the 1990s) but a Russian Orthodox church in London has existed since the late 1600s. The Cathedral of the Nativity of the Most Holy Mother of God has been beautifully designed in keeping with the Pskov School of Architecture, famous for buildings with simple domes, porches and belfries. It is a square white box with minute arched windows, a lofty Italianate bell tower and much tasteful exterior timber decoration. The building is attached to a second much older building that was once the home of Harold Sanderson (q.v.), now used as a church hall. The interior walls are lined with

Right: The Russian Orthodox
Cathedral. (© A. McMurdo)

Below: The Russian Orthodox
Cathedral. (© A. McMurdo)

The Russian
Orthodox
Cathedral.
(© A. McMurdo)

stunning colourful frescoes and the cathedral's iconostasis, the highly decorated screen that runs the width of the church in front of the altar, dominates the room. Unusually, there are very few seats as Orthodox Christians traditionally stand to worship.

Stations: Kew Bridge and Gunnersbury

50. Chiswick Park, No. 566 Chiswick High Road

Chiswick Park is a remarkably successful commercial business park sited just a few moments away from Gunnersbury station. Ever since redevelopment of this brownfield site began in 1999 the park has won continuous accolades for its construction and architecture and each year from 2011 to 2016 Chiswick Park featured in the *Financial Times'* annual 'Top 50 Places to Work'. Designed by leading architects Rogers Stirk Harbour & Partners, the business park's buildings, landscaping, environmental sustainability, performance spaces and range of leisure facilities have put it at the very forefront of London's industrial parks. In many respects it has the appearance of a university campus, with its twelve modern blocks encircling a lake, pond, public space and beautifully landscaped parkland. With its abundance of cafés, fast food outlets, a restaurant and bar

Chiswick Park. (© A. McMurdo)

it is impossible to go hungry here. Most people arrive at Chiswick Park on foot, bicycle or by public transport, although there is parking available beneath the office buildings.

From the time it was conceived the park was designed to be available to its 9,000 workers and the local community. Drop by on many a weekend or in school holidays and you will find the park buzzing with families enjoying themed days such as adventure sports and charity fundraising events. Throughout the year Enjoy-Work, the management company running the park, puts on an amazing programme of activities including classes and workshops, firework displays and major sport screenings. Recently, the Summer in the Park festival saw the arrival of deckchairs and a sandy beach, as well as a beach volleyball court, all of which proved extremely popular.

Chiswick Park is now home to more than sixty-five companies including those in entertainment, technology, media and food and drink. Many of them have based their UK or European headquarters here including Singapore Airlines, Intelsat, Sony, Starbucks, Disney, Paramount, Pepsico and Ericsson. The park's superb location, close to several stations, major transport routes and Heathrow Airport, as well as its attractive work conditions, make it all the more appealing. It is undoubtedly one of West London's most successful ventures with facilities that rival both Canary Wharf and Paddington Waterside.

Stations: Gunnersbury and Chiswick Park

Above: Chiswick Park. (© A. McMurdo)

Below: Chiswick Park. (© A. McMurdo)

About the Author

Lucy McMurdo is a modern history graduate and native Londoner who has lived in the capital all her life. In 2003 when she qualified as a London Blue Badge Tourist Guide she combined two of her major loves – history and London – and has been sharing her knowledge of the city with local and foreign visitors ever since. Always keen to explore and learn about London's secrets, she spends many hours 'walking the streets' looking out for hidden corners, unusual curiosities as well as architecturally significant buildings and ones that have a story to tell.

Lucy's tour-guiding career began over thirty years ago when she first guided overseas visitors around the UK. Since then, in addition to tour guiding she has been greatly involved in training and examining the next generation of tour guides. She has created, taught and run courses in London's University of Westminster and City University and also developed guide-training programmes for the warders and site guides at Hampton Court Palace.

Most recently Lucy has been writing about the city she is so passionate about and is the author of four London guidebooks: *Bloomsbury in 50 Buildings, Explore London's Square Mile, Streets of London* and *London in 7 Days.*

Acknowledgements

The author and publisher would like to thank the many people and organisations that have helped in the production of this book and to once again acknowledge the vital part played by the author's husband, Alex McMurdo, to whom most of the images in the book are credited. In addition to his role as photographer he has also been a wonderful sounding-off board as I vacillated between including or omitting a building, which was no easy task. I am further indebted to him and Jo for taking the time to proofread the text and give critical feedback! Particular thanks are owed to James Marshall and Adam Grounds at Hounslow Archives and Local Studies Service for their invaluable advice and help in locating relevant sources. I am also extremely grateful for help and assistance given to me by the Chiswick House and Gardens Trust, William Hogarth Trust, Fuller's, Asahi Europe Ltd, Christ Church, Turnham Green, Food & Fuel, Fusion at Chiswick Town Hall, St Michael and All Angels Church, the Old Cinema, Our Lady of Grace and St Edward Church, and the Cathedral of the Nativity of the Most Holy Mother of God and the Royal Martyrs (Russian Orthodox Cathedral).

The author would also like to thank Amberley Publishing for commissioning this book, and to acknowledge the excellent support and hard work of Angeline Wilcox, Jenny Stephens, Marcus Pennington and the whole production team.

The following may be useful for information on Chiswick:

www.brentfordandchiswicklhs.org.uk
www.historicengland.org.uk
www.british-history.ac.uk
www.chiswickcalendar.co.uk
www.chiswickw4.com.com
www.emerywalker.org.uk
www.hidden-london.com
www.hounslow.gov.uk/site
www.londonist.com
www.londonremembers.com/memorials
www.panoramaofthethames.com
www.secret-london.co.uk